FLASHES OF

Original title: Einstein e le macchine del tempo
Texts and illustrations by Luca Novelli
Graphic design by Studio Link (www.studio-link.it)

www.editorialescienza.it
www.giunti.it

English edition published in the USA by
Chicago Review Press Incorporated
814 North Franklin Street
Chicago, Illinois 60610
ISBN 978-1-61373-865-8

Library of Congress Cataloging-in-Publication Data
Is available from the Library of Congress.

Printed in the United States of America
5 4 3 2 1

Luca Novelli

Einstein and the Time Machine

CHICAGO REVIEW PRESS

THE UNIVERSE BY DEFINITION CONTAINS EVERYTHING THAT EXISTS.
EXAGGERATION!

Contents

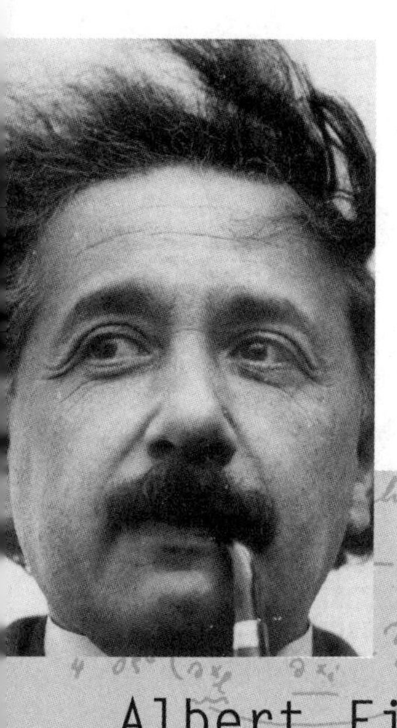

Albert Einstein

Albert Einstein was the most important scientist of the 20th century. He was grumpy but likeable. He didn't like science fiction because he considered it phony: too many novelists had twisted the deep meaning of his theories. Instead he believed in spreading knowledge, even though he never had time to write a children's book. When he wrote or spoke, he was clear, concise, and interesting—he left hundreds of letters, writings, and speeches.

This book sets out to tell of Einstein's life with full respect for his thoughts, but also playing with themes that revolutionized humankind's perceptions of time, space, and the universe. The following pages have been written as if Einstein himself was telling us about the various stages of his life, as a child, a young man, and as a grand old man, when he thought about relativity while stroking his cat, Tiger.

WHAT YOU'LL FIND IN THIS BOOK

There's me, Albert Einstein, telling my story.

And there's the story of my life, starting with when I played the violin as a child.

There's my theory about the relativity of time.

TICK TOCK
TICK TOCK
TICK

There are my discoveries about matter and energy.

There are my successes and my beliefs.

And there are the time machines—true and false, possible and impossible. All aboard. We're off!

BIG
BANG!

Our universe began with a huge explosion called the Big Bang. Everything that exists and will exist began with that explosion, even what this book is made of, and the time that it takes to read through it.

Time machines are devices capable of allowing us to travel back and forth in time. Usually you come across them in novels and adventure films, comics, and stories. The first time machine was conceived by a British writer, H. G. Wells, who was a teacher and journalist. His novel, *The Time Machine*, had an immediate and long lasting success. Since it was published, hundreds of other time machines have been imagined and described. Some of them, at least in theory, could even work. This book too, in its own way, is a kind of time machine.

1. Me, Albert Einstein

I'm sure you already know my name. Everyone in your time knows who Albert Einstein is.

Often I hear myself called "the greatest scientist in history." I assure you that I find this a little embarrassing. I don't think that I have any special talents, I'm just passionately curious. I'm wise in the sense that I work on being wise.

Wealth and success have never been important to me. Instead, love, beauty, and truth have enlightened my life, and they give me courage and happiness. I don't have superhuman powers and if it rains I can't make it stop raining. I've even told my cat that.

I was born at home in Ulm, Germany, on March 14, 1879. I arrived two years before Maja, my little sister. My mom, Pauline, is a big woman who wears a bodice made of whalebone and my dad, Hermann, has a wonderful handlebar moustache.

I was born the same year the first electric light bulb was invented. In the United States, Thomas Alva Edison managed to keep it alight for 13½ hours—a record. But it is also a rarity, because houses are still lit—badly—with gas lamps or smelly oil lamps.

I grow up with the spread of electric lighting, which had quite an impact on the first part of my life. In fact, my dad, together with my uncle Jakob, is the co-owner of an electrical company that provides electricity to the nearby town of Schwabing. And Uncle Jakob has designed a new type of dynamo.

At home I often hear them talk about physics, devices, and electricity. They are popular topics, just as computers and computer science are in 2017.

My dad wants me to become a civil engineer. And, in fact, as a child I'm interested in physics, geometry, and mathematics. But in 1895, when I take the entrance exam for the Zurich Polytechnic—me, Albert Einstein—I'm not admitted.

Mechanical clocks, the predecessors of wristwatches, are a fairly recent invention in the long history of humankind. The first were called "monastic awakeners" because they were used in the monasteries of the middle ages. They were devices that had a little bell that woke the monk in charge of ringing the church bells in the morning. But some "awakeners" were a bit more brisk: at the chosen time, containers filled with ice-cold water were tipped over the sleeping victim.

Mechanical watches have evolved over the centuries, becoming ever more precise. But clocks that are even more precise are needed to measure time in space. Today, astronomers use atomic clocks.

2. A Childhood Genius

I'm not very bright as a child. It may seem incredible, but I, one of the fathers of modern physics, am considered a bit dense. This is because I'm still not talking at four years old, and at nine I struggle to hold a conversation using the right words.

And yet, at five years old I am already good at the violin: I can play Mozart, Bach, and Schubert.

I think in pictures, the psychologists would say. I also can find my way through the tangled streets of Munich, where my family has moved. And I'm very good at creating complex structures with colored wooden cubes, the predecessors of the LEGO bricks of your time. Together with the violin, these are my favorite hobbies. There's no television, radio, comics, or video games—they don't even exist.

AAARGH!
JUST INVENT THEM ALREADY!

BANG!

At home we have just a handful of illustrated books, colored by hand. Uncle Jakob tells me stories and helps me with my homework. "Algebra," he says, "is a happy science, where you hunt for a mysterious animal we call X."

But Uncle Jakob is not the only one who talks to me about science. A student named Max Talmey comes to our house. He's a poor Jewish medical student. My family is not rich, but as is customary among the well-to-do Jews in Munich, every Friday we invite someone less fortunate than ourselves for dinner: Max, in fact. And every time, he brings me a new book to read and look at. They're all books about science. Reading these books, I start to ask the first questions about how the universe works.

OK, BUT WHAT IS THE UNIVERSE?

There are many schools of thought about when our universe was created. Current science says it was about 14 billion years ago, but for more than two centuries the date suggested by Archbishop Ussher, who lived in the 17th century, was believed to be correct. Ussher, studying the Bible in his own way, had concluded that the universe was created by God on Sunday, October 23, 4004 BC, at nine o'clock in the morning.

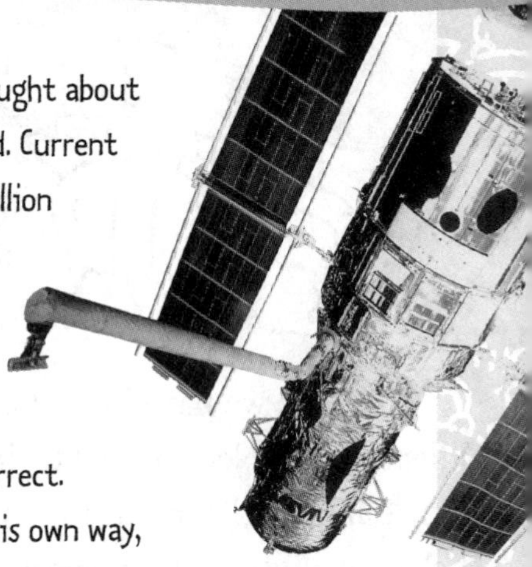

To measure the age of the universe, modern scientists have used several methods. They've studied the universe's expansion, trying to trace it back to the initial moment. They've examined meteorites and the things hidden inside them, and they've studied ancient star clusters that were formed shortly after the Big Bang. All of these methods have achieved similar results.

The Hubble Space Telescope, which was launched into orbit around the Earth in 1990, also has been used to calculate the age of the universe.

3. A Small Free Thinker

The Bible is extraordinarily important to me for a few years during my childhood. It's a wonderful book that tells the story of my people and our relationship with God. It uses grand images: paradise lost, seas that divide, angels that descend to earth, people turned into salt statues, and cities destroyed by rains of fire.

I go to a Catholic school and I'm the only Jew in my class. The lessons of the Torah—of the Jewish faith—are given to me at home by a relative.

I'm so passionate about the Old Testament that I become even more religious than my parents, who are less interested.

Then, once I started reading the science books that my friend Max brought me, I began looking at the stories in the Bible with a scientific eye. They can't all be taken literally! And so I become a kind of free thinker, convinced that the young are intentionally kept in a cloud of ignorance and lies.

At 12 years old I find myself clashing with everything and everyone: widely held beliefs, authority figures, and most especially school and some teachers. I hate wearing a uniform and marching, which we young Prussians are obliged to do on Fridays, Saturdays, and Sundays. I hate learning things by repetition. Because of this, my Greek professor says I'll never achieve anything of value in my life.

Even my own family doesn't think much of me. When my dad decides to move to Italy to open a new business, he shuts up our house and leaves me alone in a Munich boarding house. I'm 15 years old. What would you have done in my place?

In reality, the galaxies and stars in our sky are no longer in the places and states in which we currently see them. The ones we see are stars and nebulae from millions and billions of years ago, the time it took for their light to reach us. The night sky is a vision of a very distant past, from the time of the dinosaurs, trilobites, and still more distant eras.

4. The First Escape

In Munich—alone and with no family—I have to finish high school and then enlist in the Prussian army.

Already I see myself marching, marching, marching, first to the Luitpold Gymnasium school along with my classmates, then on to Germany. I'm so depressed that I manage to get a medical certificate claiming I've had a nervous breakdown. I give it to the school. The headmaster reads it, then looks at me and expels me . . . rather, he "leaves me free to drop out of school."

I pack my bags and, with my violin, I travel across the Alps. I join my mom, dad, my sister Maja, and my uncle Jakob in Italy.

In Munich I left nothing behind. The big house where we lived had been sold to a builder, who cut down all the old trees in the garden and turned the property into a condominium.

My classmates were already strangers to me. More and more, the city was crowded with marching troops. Even my Greek teacher told me it was best to leave. He thinks I'm too negative and disrespectful.

But I'm also curious: my cousins who live in Genoa have told me that some parts of Italy are just like paradise on earth. I want to see the sea, to enjoy the sun and my family.

BERLIN
ULM
MUNICH
PRAGUE
BERN
AARU
ZURICH
MILAN
PAVIA
MEDITERRANEAN
SEA

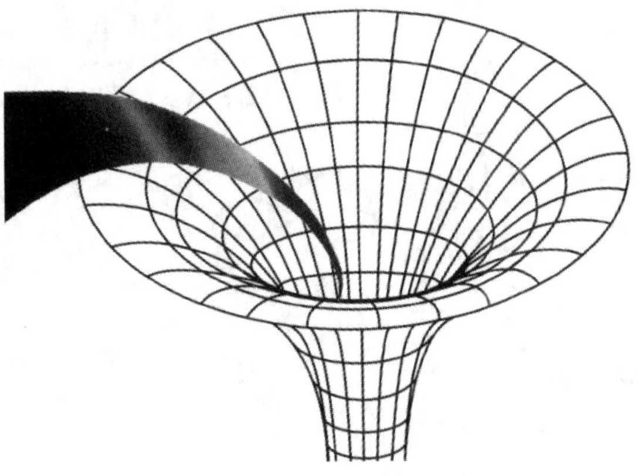

Even Mark Twain (author of *The Adventures of Tom Sawyer*) described a journey through time in one of his novels from 1889. He didn't imagine strange contraptions, but he enjoyed plunging one of his characters into King Arthur's court, with all the complications that came along with that.

This idea of portals—holes or tunnels that open into the past or into the future—is no longer just imagination. Modern physics does not exclude the possibility of time travel, and calls these portals in time "space-time tunnels."

5. Holiday in Italy

So I arrive in Pavia, a small town on the river Ticino with a beautiful central square and many medieval buildings.

The river running through it is not big, but it's large enough to be navigated by small boats. Large barges go back and forth along the Naviglio, the canal linking Pavia to Milan.

I've always liked water. As a child I had fun with my toy boats in the bathtub. When I grow up, sailing is my only hobby. I buy a boat the size of a walnut shell, which I call *Tinnef*, Yiddish for "junk." I like sailing as a sport because it's not too much hard work.

In Pavia, my family lives in an important house, where the famous poet Ugo Foscolo once lived.

It's summer and the weather is mild, but I don't really like the people who visit our house. Especially the ladies—corseted and stiff like they've swallowed a broomstick. They want to make me play the violin the way they like it, rather than how I like to play it. I play and keep quiet. It's the best way to make music!

My dad doesn't pay much attention to me. In fact, he's very irritated with me as I left Munich against his wishes. He wants me to attend the Zurich Polytechnic and says that here in Italy there are no schools that would suit me. I'm an unexpected nuisance for him.

And at the moment, he doesn't want any other problems because he's building a power plant with Uncle Jakob and other associates. It'll be the first here in Pavia.

In short, my dad doesn't want me around. So he sends me to take the entrance exam at the Zurich Polytechnic and gets me recommended. Even if I don't really want to; even if it's too early.

GO, AND COME BACK AN ENGINEER ON THE DOUBLE!

What year is it? What day is it? What time is it? It's easy to say, just take a look at the clock and calendar. What's much more difficult to say is what time actually is.

You might be happy with this definition: time is a concept that allows us to distinguish between events—which takes place first, second, and so on. We pass through time. First we are children, then adults, and then finally old people. But it is also true that time "moves with us," and it moves in space. If we take a train journey, as we move through space we also move in time. At the end of the trip we are a little bit older. Time and space are two closely related concepts.

6. Failed!

Einstein in German means "one stone." But I, "Albert One Stone," am not at all made of stone. Instead I am very upset that I haven't passed the entrance exam to the Polytechnic.

I'm upset even though I took the test two years earlier than normal, at the age of 16, and not at 18 as required. The principal called me a "child prodigy" and I was quite hurt.

Now I'm at the local school in Aarau, Switzerland, to prepare myself while waiting for the two years to pass until I can be admitted to the Polytechnic.

I miss my family a bit, especially my mom and sister, Maja, but still I consider myself lucky. I'm a guest of the Winteler family, lovely people. Mr. Jost Winteler is a Greek teacher, but he knows all about birds. He even talks to them; he trills and chirps. Basically he's an amateur ornithologist.

Mrs. Winteler is a good cook and is very kind to me. And then there's the prettiest of his three daughters, who's a little older than me. I play the piano in a duet with her, which I really enjoy.

When I'm with her, time passes so fast. Yesterday I saw a ray of sun touch her hair and I thought it was a beautiful sight.

What a strange thing light is! What a strange thing time is!

WHAT STRANGE THINGS WOMEN ARE.

Switzerland is a country of clocks and the Swiss are proud of their accuracy. Clocks, above all, are time machines. They don't stop time, they don't make time go forward or backward, but they measure it, and without bias. Yet two identical clocks, even very precise Swiss ones, if wound up at the same time in two different places in the universe, will show different times after a while.

All clocks have an oscillating system which gives them the rhythm of time. In pendulum clocks, this system is the pendulum. In balance wheel clocks, it's the balance wheel. The clock's precision depends on the regularity of these oscillations. In atomic clocks the oscillators are vibrating atoms. The margin of error for time determined by an atomic clock is 1 second every 3 million years! Using these clocks, it has been possible carry out some experimental tests on Einstein's theory.

7. The First Time for Albert

Aarau is a very pretty Swiss village. You can go on beautiful walks in the nearby mountains, and the view from the Alps is extraordinary! I feel very good here.

The Winteler family is wonderful, there's always a feast at the table, and—most important—Marie likes me. She's always very affectionate toward me.

The school that I attend is not at all bad, and there's a new and very well equipped physics lab. This is where I first think about how nice it would be to follow a ray of sunshine.

Now I'm in Zurich, and I'm all alone. I've been enrolled at the Polytechnic since October. I passed the exams. I even gave up my German citizenship and I am currently stateless, without a country. My father is troubled by this. For him, "stateless" is almost an insult.

During school holidays, first from Aarau and then from Zurich, I often visited him in Milan, where he had moved his business and our family. Now he lives in a street not far from the Duomo and the Piazza della Scala, in an old mansion owned by a countess. I walk around the city and in the Galleria, and I buy German newspapers.

I also took a trip to Genoa, where I visited my cousins. It was a wonderful trip. I crossed the Apennines on foot, all the way to the sea. And there I saw an extraordinary vision: so many colorful houses with lush vegetation overlooking the water that stretched out endlessly. And then the light. . . . I'd never seen such a light!

Light is the thing that makes it possible to see things. Its secret nature has always fascinated mankind.

Even Einstein asks himself at age 16, "What would I see if I traveled on a beam of light?" In Einstein's time, some scientists thought that light is made up of tiny, individual particles, while others, who were in the majority, argued that it behaves like a continuous electromagnetic wave.

Einstein doesn't solve the problem completely, but he believes that light has characteristics of both particles and waves. In fact, light behaves like a continuous wave when it forms a rainbow in the sky, and like a group of tiny, individual packets of energy when, for example, you turn on a lightbulb. Its speed, though, is the one thing that never changes. It's always constant at any point in the universe: 186,000 miles/sec (300,000 km/sec).

8. Einstein in Love

I'm now a young man. I attend the Zurich Polytechnic and I've grown a nice moustache. I've also met a girl called Mileva, who is three and a half years older than me. She's from Vojvodina, in Serbia, and lives in a home for female students, far from her family. She's good—she thinks about her exams and studies hard. We study calculus, geometry, and physics together. We eat pounds of sausages and drink gallons of coffee together.

When I vacation back home in Italy, I write her affectionate letters, but I also talk to her about molecules and gases. Mileva helps me write my first scientific paper, which is about capillary action, the way that fluids behave around solids.

I want to marry her, but we don't have any money, not even to buy two bikes to go riding in the countryside. And besides, my parents are against our relationship. But I'll marry her anyway, I've already decided.

We also vacation together. We arranged to meet in Como, Italy, hopped on a boat, and visited Villa Carlotta, strolling through its park.

I really need to get a job in order to marry Mileva. But the only possibility I can see is to get hired as a clerk in the patent office in Bern. I still look for other jobs. I apply to universities all over Europe, from Stuttgart to Pisa, and also to an insurance company and to a boarding school.

As a promising young physicist, I've already invented an interesting theory about electrons. But I'm unemployed and without a penny in my pocket. I give private math lessons, but I'd earn more playing my violin on the street. I haven't ruled that out!

Science fiction is full of interstellar travel that ends up with something unexpected. The astronaut leaves for a distant star and reaches speeds close to that of light, 186,000 miles per sec (300,000 km/sec). But in interstellar space, time flows more slowly. When the space traveler returns to our planet, only a few months have gone by for him, but centuries have gone by for those still on Earth. The traveler's loved ones have already been dust for generations. The astronaut has made a leap in time, because his spaceship works like a time machine.

It's not just science fiction; it's an effect of relativity.

9. Einstein the Inventor

I'm in Bern. I've been working at the patent office since June 16, 1902, as a third-level technical expert, temporarily and on probation. It's an easy job, what I call a "cobbler's job," with all due respect to cobblers.

Some of the strangest projects and the most unusual people come into the office. For each new invention, its originality and intention needs to be determined.

I myself have some patents to my name, for a hearing aid and a refrigerator that makes no noise.

NOW I'M SWISS!
TOCK
TICK
TICK
TOCK

Bern is a nice city, and I'm comfortable here. I've become a Swiss citizen, but I won't have to serve in the military because I have been rejected . . . for flat feet.

Together with some friends I founded the Olympia Academy, of which I am the honorary president. The purpose of this group is to talk about physics and eat well.

And I finally married Mileva. Now we live in an apartment in the center of town, close to the clock tower.

TO SCIENCE!

She helps me with my studies, but she becomes a full-time mother when Hans, our first child, is born. She was already overburdened with laundry and dishes to clean, but now she also has diapers to boil and baby food to cook.

Even among the drying laundry, baby bottles, and the squeals of little Hans, I manage to write sheet after sheet. On them, the most revolutionary scientific ideas in human history take shape, those of my theory of relativity.

Time and space are relative. Imagine you're on a train moving at 50 meters per second, and that your friend is stationary outside the train, observing what you're doing. Roll a marble in the aisle of the train in the same direction that the train moves. For you, still on the train, your ball is moving at 2 meters per second. For your friend, who is watching you from a stationary position outside of the train, your marble moves at 52 meters per second, the train speed plus the speed of the marble.

According to the theory of relativity, to a stationary or slow-moving observer, the faster you go past, the more time slows down. Albert Einstein gives an example of a man walking with his dog: the man walks slowly, while the dog goes back and forth, constantly wagging his tail. At the end of the walk, while the man has walked a few miles, the dog has done more and aged less than his owner. Not only that, the dog's tail has aged less than the tip of its nose.

MY TAIL IS TWO MINUTES BEHIND.

10. The Theory of Relativity (Special Relativity)

It's 1905. I'm 26 and work at the patent office, but I still think about physics. And I continue to fill notebooks with formulas.

I publish my theories in a newspaper for professionals, *Annalen der Physik*, run by Max Planck. In the first article, which I send to the magazine three days after my birthday, I demonstrate that light, while having the same properties as electromagnetic waves, is actually made up of tiny particles.

In the second article I explain a mysterious molecular movement that had been observed by Robert Brown, which he called Brownian motion.

In the third article, which I send out in June, I show that space and time are relative to the observer.

THE RULER APPEARS TO SHRINK DEPENDING ON THE OBSERVER
THE CLOCK TICKS MORE SLOWLY
TICK
TOCK
DEPENDING ON THE OBSERVER

Space contracts as you approach the speed of light. A moving clock measures time more slowly than the watch on the wrist of the observer. It's what Max Planck will call the Theory of Relativity.

"The minute is in danger!" screams a Viennese newspaper headline, commenting on my article.

In September I send the Annalen der Physik another article that definitively revolutionizes the concepts of matter and energy.

This relationship between energy and mass is defined by the famous formula: $E = mc^2$.

Energy = mass x the speed of light squared. The speed of light (c) is constant, and very fast: 186,000 miles per hour (300,000 km per second). A mass (M), even a very small one, multiplied by the enormous value of the speed of light *twice*, releases a huge amount of energy (E). The atomic bomb is based on this concept, but Einstein hadn't thought of that yet.

Small amounts of matter can be turned into large amounts of energy. In nuclear power plants, radioactive fuel mass (uranium or plutonium) is converted into heat energy.

11. Einstein Misunderstood

Nothing. For a few years after having posed the Theory of Relativity (which will be called "Special Relativity"), nothing changes in my life. It seems that no one cares about my theory, especially the physicists. In fact, when I present it together with a job application at the University of Bern, it's called "incomprehensible" by the chair of theoretical physics.

The worst is that they don't hire me. So, for several years, I keep working at the patent office. Basically I'm considered an "amateur scientist" by everyone, even if in 1906 I earned a doctorate at the University of Zurich.

Something new: the patent office promotes me to being a second-level technical expert. This is good—some extra money for the family.

It's not until three years after publishing a theory that will revolutionize modern physics that I finally become an official member of the scientific community: in 1908 I become a "private teacher" at the University of Bern. In this job, I teach lessons for a few students and friends.

Meanwhile, while working at the patent office, I look out of the window and see something fall in front of me. I have an idea: if something falls freely, it doesn't feel its own weight, that is, it doesn't weigh anything. It's easily proven, and I'm not saying that you have to throw yourself out the window with a bathroom scale. All you have to do is watch an astronaut inside a spaceship orbiting the Earth, basically "falling" toward the planet in a circle.

What can I conclude from that? That gravity and acceleration are equivalent. I have a feeling that my Theory of Relativity has to be . . . expanded.

Albert Einstein says that time also changes in relation to gravity in space. The more you are attracted by gravity toward a body, the more time slows down. The greater the mass of the body, the stronger the attraction, and the slower time runs. So, time is slower on the surface of Jupiter than it is on Earth. And even slower on the surface of the sun or a bigger star. Not to mention black holes, where time stops altogether.

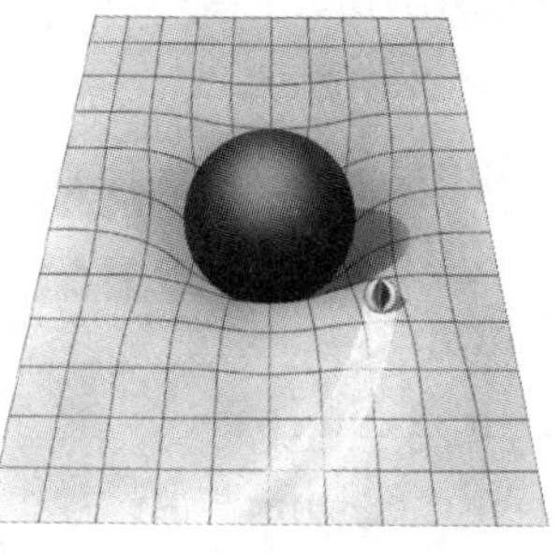

Gravity is a force that causes attraction between bodies. To understand how gravity and mass react in space, imagine space is a thin sheet of rubber, and imagine placing a heavy object on it. The object will sink into the sheet and cause a depression that's as deep as the object is heavy. But outer space also has a time dimension. Therefore, mass warps space-time.

FINALLY, YOU HAVE AN EXCUSE FOR ALL YOUR TARDINESS.
HELP!

12. Now I'm a Professor

In 1909 I meet my first real physicists at the Salzburg Physics Conference. Finally, I stop being an amateur among amateurs. In May of the same year, the University of Zurich gives me a job: Associate Professor of Theoretical Physics.

I am confident about this new job, but to be careful, I wait until June to resign from the patent office. Never burn bridges until you're sure you've reached the other side.

Mileva gives birth to our second son, Eduard. With two children to look after, I realize I need to build a career: there's never enough money for the family! So I accept a position at the German University in Prague. It's quite far from all my loved ones, but it's a great opportunity. I move to Prague with the whole family.

Prague is a beautiful city but it's part of the Austro-Hungarian Empire. The various ethnicities—Germans, Czechs, Jews—look at each other with distrust. The city is gloomy and rather dirty. At home we have to battle with fleas!

On the plus side, the food is very good. The university uniform fits me perfectly, and it makes me look like an admiral.

There's a very well equipped lab where I can experiment and work on my theories. Here I come up with another idea: if light—as I said—has a mass, it means it is attracted to larger masses.

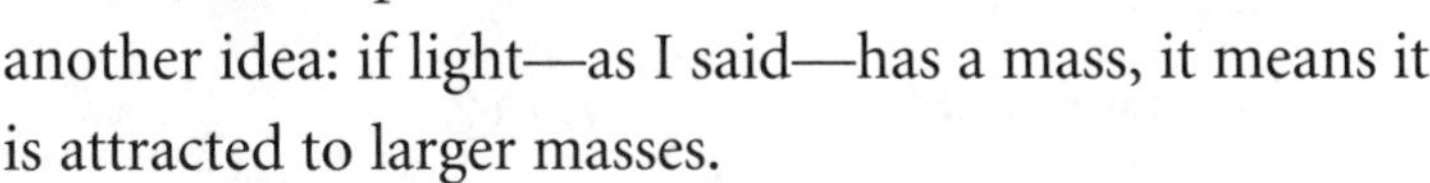

I ask my astronomer friends about it. They say I'm right: the light from the stars is deflected by the sun.

Black holes were stars, like our sun. At a certain point they exploded, and then they collapsed into an enormously large mass nucleus. A teaspoon of atoms from a black hole would be equivalent to the mass of an aircraft carrier. The force of gravity from a collapsed star is so strong that not even light manages to get away from it. That is the reason it is called a "black hole." It neither emits nor reflects light, it only attracts light. In fact, a black hole attracts everything, even time, which becomes very slow near it, until time stops altogether. However precise a clock, if thrown into a black hole, it would never strike twelve.

Time would also stop for an astronaut (or tourist) who ended up near a black hole. Also, both the clock and the tourist would be pulled into very long spaghetti strands by the enormous force of gravity.

13. Everybody Wants Me!

COME TO US!
COME TO US!
L

The wind is changing for me. The universities of Utrecht, Vienna, and Leiden each offer me a job. Even the Zurich Polytechnic calls me, where until recently I was considered an amateur. And that's the one I accept. I return to Zurich with my family.

Now I'm studying geometry, not that of Euclid, but that of a certain Dr. Riemann, who imagines a world where two parallel things cannot always be parallel, and where even the right angles of a square are curved. With a square and a compass it's rather difficult to describe it, but with equations you can explore it. Many mathematicians have done it before me, without any precise results.

α
β
γ

Instead, I think that the universe is a complete whole of space and time, and that it can be described using this geometry where everything—sooner or later—curves.

Max Planck offers me a Chair at the Royal Prussian Academy of Sciences in Berlin. I can't refuse, because it has become the most important research center in the world.

Unfortunately, war breaks out—the Great War, as it will be called later. It grows out of all proportion, with unprecedented violence in the name of a patriotism that I don't share.

Terrible things happen. A colleague of mine at the University of Berlin has even tested deadly gas on the eastern front.

The enemy could have been the one to first use gas, it wouldn't have changed a thing. War is not a parlor game in which the players respect the rules. Life and death are at stake. The only way to eliminate the horrors of war is to totally reject it.

The universe can be thought of as an enormous expanding sausage. Every object that it contains, as well as the universe itself, can be described through three dimensions (height, width, and depth) that change over time.

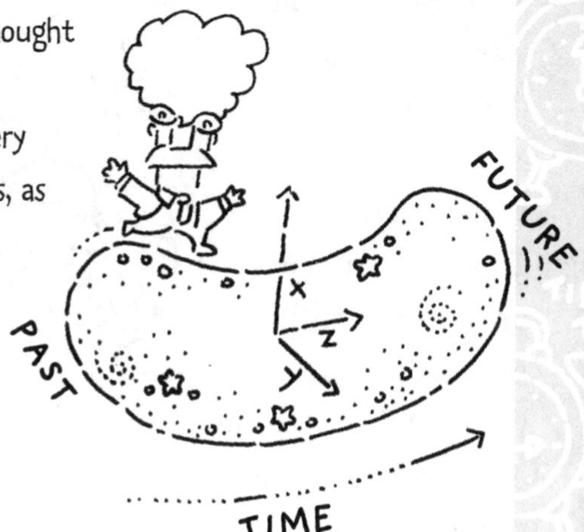

Our universe has four dimensions. It stretches out uninterrupted in space and time. Physicists call this a "space-time continuum." According to the Theory of Relativity, gravity bends this "continuum" as well as the universe itself.

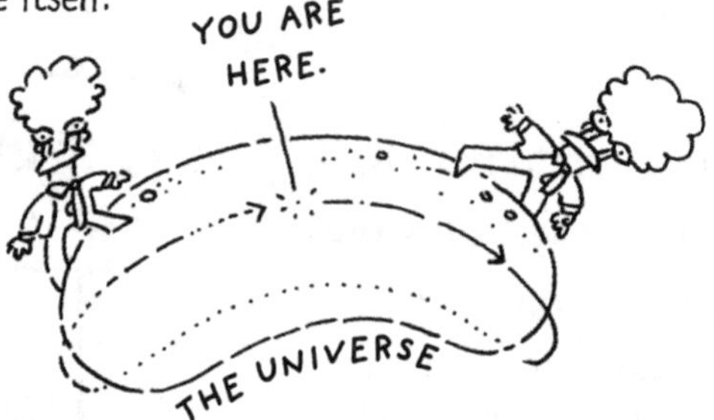

The universe is so curved, that if it were possible to walk from one side to the other, you would find yourself at the point at which you departed. Of course it would be a little trip of several billion years. Good luck!

14. The Mystery of Mercury

The conflict in Europe spreads. The war is increasingly brutal and pointless.

I'm still working on the General Theory of Relativity. I believe that gravity is not simply a force exerted on a body by another, but a property of our universe, of the "space-time continuum." All objects with a large mass create distortions in the space and time around them. I can prove it thanks to Mercury

Mercury is the closest planet to the sun. It behaves in a way that generations of astronomers have called bizarre. Its orbit seems not to obey the laws of physics. Some astronomers even hypothesized that there must be an unseen planet affecting it: Vulcan (later home to Dr. Spock from *Star Trek*). Was this science fiction planet to blame for altering the orbit of Mercury so . . . bizarrely?

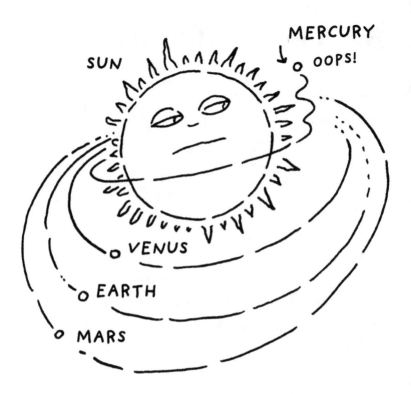

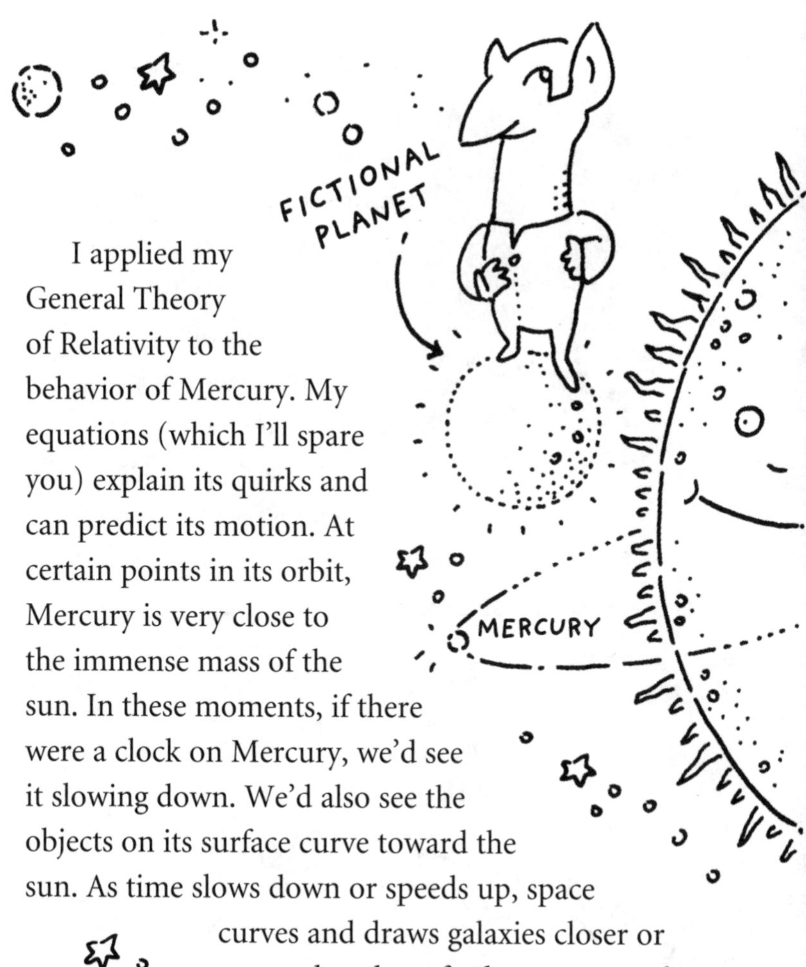

I applied my General Theory of Relativity to the behavior of Mercury. My equations (which I'll spare you) explain its quirks and can predict its motion. At certain points in its orbit, Mercury is very close to the immense mass of the sun. In these moments, if there were a clock on Mercury, we'd see it slowing down. We'd also see the objects on its surface curve toward the sun. As time slows down or speeds up, space curves and draws galaxies closer or pushes them farther away . . . these are things that happen in many places in the universe.

According to the General Theory of Relativity, the universe is curved upon itself. In this universe, two parts of it—one from the past and the other from the future—could come into contact with each other, making a shortcut possible, a space-time tunnel. The Starship *Enterprise* from *Star Trek*—science fiction for now—sometimes travels through tunnels like this, tunnels that are theoretically possible.

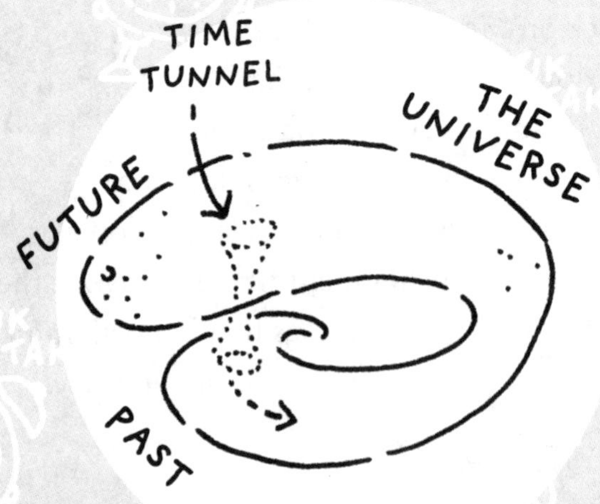

15. The Nobel Prize

The Great War is over—finally, the guns fall silent. People are very happy, and they are interested in relativity. The *New York Times* and the major newspapers in Europe write about it. Relativity is becoming as popular as the Charleston.

My relationship with Mileva, my first wife, has gotten worse. I'm sad for the children, but I divorce her. I go to live in Berlin with my future second wife, Elsa, already a mother of two little girls.

As I love food, I put on some weight. I've became a public figure, and I meet important people, so I have to be a bit more careful how I dress. I also become friends with Charlie Chaplin.

In 1921 I receive the Nobel Prize for Physics, curiously not for my Theory of Relativity, but for discovering the photoelectric effect. It's almost a consolation prize, but it's accompanied by a check for $32,000. I give it to my children and my first wife. I think they deserve it.

Now my life could be serene and pleasant. My work and career are going well, and I've bought a cottage on a lake near Berlin. But unfortunately, here in Germany something terrible is happening: the Jews are accused of being the cause of all the country's problems. Hitler has risen to power. In the square they burn the books containing ideas that the Nazi regime doesn't like. The Theory of Relativity is one of them.

At the university there are those who attack the "Jewish physics" (that is, my theory) and Hitler's Brownshirts raid my house on the lake, turning everything upside down.

Luckily I'm abroad on a conference tour with my wife and her daughters, so I return instead to Belgium. Then I decide to accept a position at the Institute of Advanced Studies at Princeton, and I leave for the United States. I never want to go back to Germany.

Albert Einstein introduced the concept of "light quantum," packets of energy particles that have the same characteristics as electromagnetic waves, thus launching the field of quantum physics or mechanics. Quantum mechanics proposes a "probabilistic" description of infinitely small particles. Matter is made up of particles that statistically are there, but that doesn't mean that they're really there. An event probably occurs at that time, but not necessarily so. Taking this concept to the extreme, the physicist Erwin Schrödinger proved that in the same universe a cat may be alive and dead at the same time.

THAT'S WHY WE CATS HAVE NINE LIVES!

16. Einstein in America

I'm not alone in seeking asylum in the United States. In the late 1930s, thousands of European scientists are forced to leave their countries, persecuted by the racist laws imposed by Hitler and his allies.

Among them are two of my physicist colleagues: the Italian Enrico Fermi and the Hungarian Leo Szilard. They never imagined that their work in the United States would change the history of planet Earth.

I feel good in America. During one of my first visits to this country I was named "The Great Relative" by a tribe of the Hopi Indians.

I decide to live in a large wooden house in Princeton, not far from the university. I live there with my wife, Elsa; her daughter Margot; my sister, Maja; and Helen Dukas, a secretary-friend who brings order to my life. I also have a dog and a cat.

I hear increasingly unsettling news from Europe: millions of people are persecuted, deported, or killed for their ideas, religion, or race.

In 1939, Hitler's Germany invades Poland. It's the beginning of World War II. Within a few months the war wreaks havoc across France, Belgium, Holland, the Balkans, and Russia, before spreading to the rest of the world.

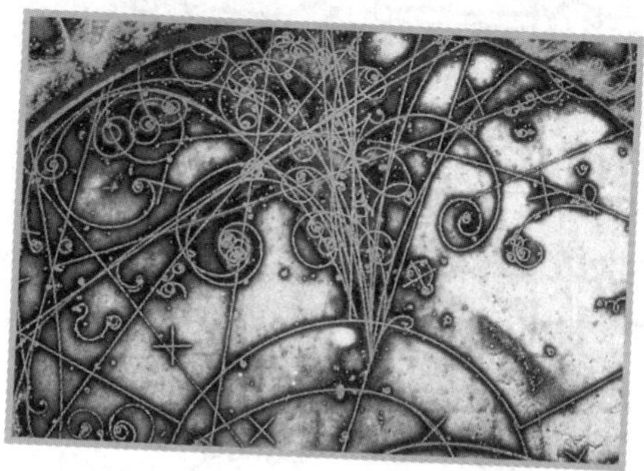

Quantum physics sees matter as composed of elementary particles that have the same properties as electromagnetic waves. Scientists have identified between 50 and 200 types, from the electron to the proton, from the graviton to the photon. Some particles behave in an extraordinary way. Some are even able to go back in time . . .

LIKE YOU
AT SCHOOL.
TIME +
TIME −

17. The Bomb

I never thought that the Theory of Relativity could have military applications. Only in 1939, after reading something by Enrico Fermi and Leo Szilard, do I sense a disturbing danger.

I know that uranium atoms can be turned into an important form of energy, and so also into a powerful and terrible weapon in the hands of the Nazis.

This leads me to write to President Franklin D. Roosevelt to urge him to be on the alert, and to invest money and research into the bomb.

In 1940, I swear allegiance to the United States in Trenton, New Jersey, and became an American citizen, although I keep my Swiss citizenship as well. I don't mind still being a bit Swiss.

Unfortunately, the world situation worsens: Japan attacks US forces stationed in the Pacific by bombing Pearl Harbor. And so, in 1941, America enters the war.

WHEN WILL IT END?
I CAN'T STAND IT ANY LONGER.
PEARL HARBOR

Enrico Fermi, together with Leo Szilard and others, build the first atomic "pile" in Chicago. The project to construct the first nuclear bomb starts with their group.

THE MANHATTAN PROJECT

I rewrite my original 1905 article on the Theory of Special Relativity by hand. The paper is auctioned and sold for $6 million. I give the proceeds to the American war effort. But I never worked on the atomic bomb and the so-called Manhattan project.

I never thought they'd manage to build a bomb small enough to be loaded onto a plane. And yet, on August 6, 1945, the radio announces that the first atomic bomb has been dropped on the Japanese city of Hiroshima.

Let's imagine for a moment that it's possible to travel back in time. You might immediately consider going back to correct the great problems of history, for example, to prevent Hitler from seizing power, therefore avoiding all the horrors that followed.

But by changing this series of events, you'd also eliminate the reason, in the future, for your journey into the past in the first place, and maybe even you.

Think, time travelers, think . . .

18. Thinking of Peace

The war is over, but peace is not what it once was. Atomic bombs are being built all over the world.

I'm still working on my Theory of Relativity. I know it's missing something, but I don't know if I'll manage to complete it . . .

In the meantime, I try to put my life and my things into order, as you would before going on a long trip. I make a will. And I make sure that all my letters and manuscripts will be donated to the Hebrew University of Jerusalem.

I've even been offered the presidency of the new State of Israel. I'm honored, but I refuse.

HERE'S EINSTEIN!
EINSTEIN SPEAKS!
FLASH!

Over the course of half a century, I've became the most famous scientist on the planet. I'm old and tired, but I'm glad to be listened to, not only for my theories but also for my opinions, especially those about nuclear weapons.

We've released the power of the atom and it has changed everything, but if we don't change our ways of thinking, we'll hurtle toward horrible disasters.

I don't know with what weapons World War III will be fought, but I do know with what ones the fourth will be fought: with axes and clubs.

For this reason, on April 11, 1955, I write to my friend Bertrand Russell, signing a manifesto that urges all nations to renounce atomic weapons.

It's my last letter. My last gesture.

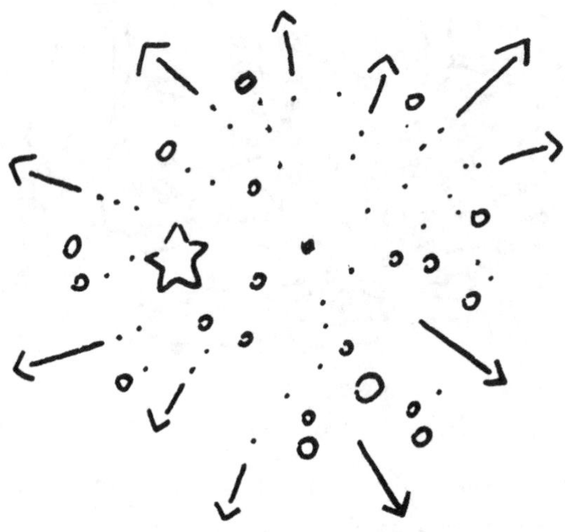

Albert Einstein left this relative time on April 18, 1955.

During his lifetime, the universe expanded further, and billions of stars were born and died. On our little planet, many new things about matter and energy have been discovered, but his theories have not been surpassed. In fact, they're still a good way of exploring the secret nature of the universe.

Albert Einstein's ashes were scattered in an unknown location. His atoms have been returned to the earth and the cosmos. His brain and eyes were removed and are still preserved in American research institutes.

Until his final day, Albert Einstein tried to complete his theory. Many others have attempted, and are still attempting to do so.

Einstein opened a door into space and time. The future—thanks to him—reserves infinite surprises.

rechnung des Ebenentensors

bleibt stehen.

zweites Glied:

Relativity Dictionary

ATOM

This was once considered the smallest indivisible part of matter. Now it's considered very much divisible into ever smaller particles, some so small and so fast that they can no longer be considered "particles" but rather packets (quanta) of energy.

AS I'VE ALWAYS SUSPECTED!

ATOMIC BOMB

This is a powerful explosive device that uses nuclear reactions to transform a small amount of matter into a large amount of energy. The name "atomic bomb" is used for three kinds of bombs: uranium, plutonium, and hydrogen. The first two make use of the phenomenon of fission, where atoms break apart, while the last uses fusion, where atoms combine. We could do without all three types.

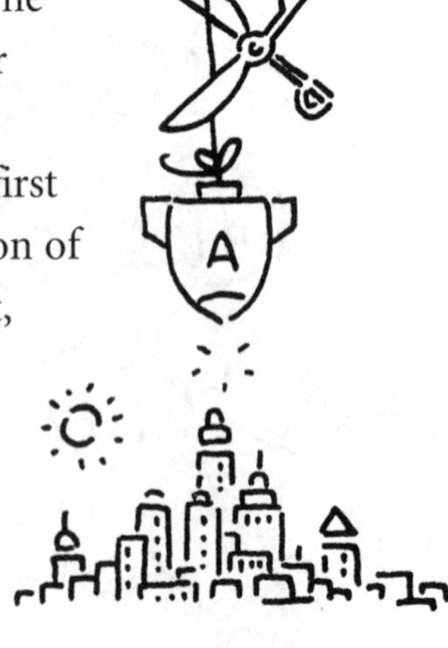
A

ATOMIC PILE

This uses a nuclear reaction, during which a small portion of matter releases an enormous amount of energy in a controlled manner. The first, built by piling up blocks of graphite and uranium, was made by Enrico Fermi in 1942 in Chicago, under the university stadium. Atomic piles are the main component of nuclear power plants.

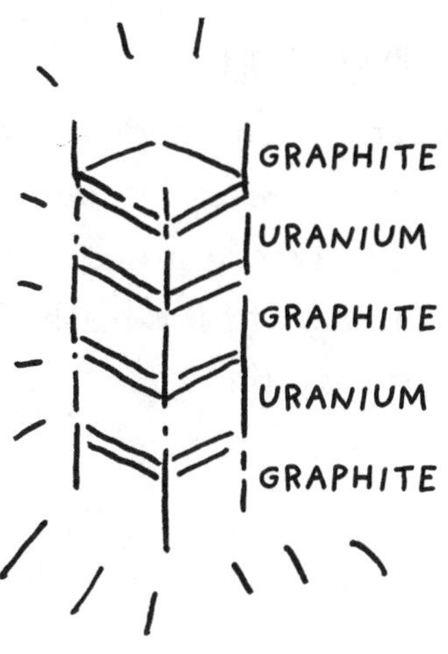

BIG BANG

This is the great explosion from which the universe was born, at least according to current theories and knowledge. When Einstein formulated his theory, the universe was considered static and infinite. The Big Bang theory is supported by the fact that all galaxies are moving away from the same single point of the universe.

BLACK HOLE

This is a former star that has exploded and collapsed in on itself, very common in the universe. Its force of gravity is so strong that it attracts everything, even light. That's why it is black. On its surface, time as we know it stands still.

BOHR, NIELS

(1885–1962) Bohr was a Danish physicist and one of the founders of quantum mechanics. He sometimes argued with his friend and colleague Albert Einstein. In the latter part of his life he tried to apply his quantum theories to life sciences.

BROWNIAN MOTION

This is the nonstop, random motion of small particles on the surface of liquids, as discovered by the Scottish naturalist Robert Brown. Einstein worked out that it was caused by the motion of the molecules of the liquid itself.

CAPILLARITY

This is a phenomenon that liquids show when in very narrow tubes. Albert Einstein studied it in his youth, together with Mileva Maric, who later became his wife.

CARICATURE

Albert Einstein was portrayed in thousands of portraits and caricatures, many very nice, some not. In the drawing below, circulated at a journalists' ball in Vienna in 1931, he is portrayed along with Freud and Steinach, both very famous doctors at that time.

COSMOS

This is the space inhabited by galaxies, stars, and planets. It's another way of saying "universe."

CURIE, MARIE

Marie Sklodowska Curie (1867–1934), was a Polish-born French physicist and chemist. Exiled in Paris, she married Pierre Curie, with whom she studied radioactivity. Albert Einstein was both her friend and colleague. In the photo here, taken in 1911 at the Solvay Conference in Brussels, Belgium, Madame Curie is the only woman. The young Albert Einstein is standing on the right.

DEMONSTRATION

A little time travel and a dramatic demonstration of the effects of the Theory of Relativity were shown by sending two groups of scientists on a tour of the world on two different aircrafts. Before departure all watches and clocks were synchronized. The first plane traveled in the direction of the Earth's rotation, to the east. The second flew in the opposite direction to the Earth's rotation, westward. Compared to the Earth, which rotated opposite in space beneath it, this plane traveled much faster. When the two groups found themselves back at the starting point, the watches and clocks in the first group were all ahead by a couple of minutes compared to those in the second group. They had traveled faster, and for them time had moved more slowly.

EINSTEIN, ALBERT

(1879–1955) As a child he was just like every other boy, quite studious but not too much. In Munich, he attended the Luitpold Gymnasium secondary school until 1894. In this class photo he is in the lower right corner

ENERGY

This comes in different forms: thermal, nuclear, mechanical, electrical, and more. It can be defined as the capacity to carry out a task. The main source of energy in the universe is the matter that, by canceling its mass, transforms itself into energy, as per Einstein's formula. All other sources of energy—including the "exploitable" ones such as solar, gravitational, and organic energy—are traceable back to that first one.

FERMI, ENRICO

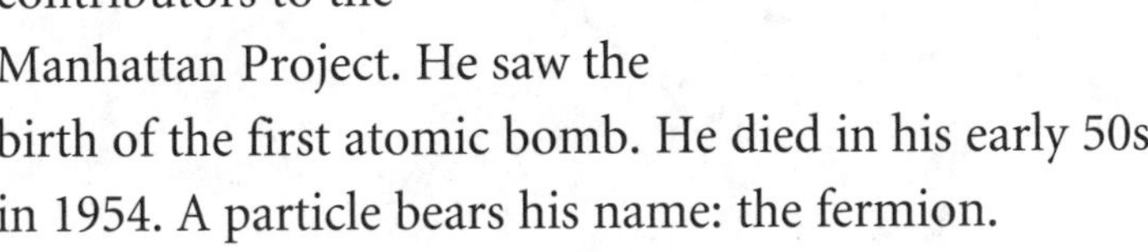

(1901–1954) An Italian physicist and 1938 Nobel Prize winner, he built the first atomic pile in Chicago, proving that the splitting of the atom was controllable. He was one of the contributors to the Manhattan Project. He saw the birth of the first atomic bomb. He died in his early 50s in 1954. A particle bears his name: the fermion.

FREUD, SIGMUND

(1856–1939). An Austrian psychiatrist and philosopher. His books were burned by Hitler's regime. Along with Einstein, he wrote the book *Why War?* in 1933.

GRAVITY

The acceleration to which all the bodies that lie in the gravitational field of a planet or any massive body are subjected to.

GREAT RELATIVE

The Hopi Indians gave Albert Einstein the title of Great Relative. Next to him is his wife, Elsa, who is smiling.

MANHATTAN PROJECT

This led to the construction of the first atomic bomb, detonated near Alamogordo, New Mexico, on July 16, 1945. On August 6 of the same year, one was dropped on the city of Hiroshima in Japan.

MASS

A measure of inertia, that is, the tendency of a body to maintain its direction and speed. It's a physical quantity that's independent from the state of the body. An astronaut has the same mass in space, where he weighs zero, as on the Earth, where he weighs 220 pounds (100 kg).

MATTER

According to classic physics, everything that has a mass is matter. But when it comes down to the infinitely small, the concept of matter is confused with that of energy.

MAXWELL, JAMES CLERK

(1831–1879) A Scottish physicist, he was the first to formulate a theory that equates light waves to electromagnetic waves. He also came up with the concept of the electromagnetic field. And he was the first to suggest that time was not the same everywhere. Einstein developed his Theory of Relativity from Maxwell's works and equations.

MILAN

Albert's father, Hermann, is buried in Milan. He died in October 1901. The Einstein family lived for several years in via Bigli, in a house owned by the Countess Clara Maffei.

NOBEL PRIZE

This prestigious award was established by the Swedish industrialist Alfred Bernhard Nobel. Albert Einstein received it for physics in 1921.

PHOTOELECTRIC EFFECT

Discovered by Albert Einstein, this is the effect by which a metal struck by light emits electrons. It confirms Einstein's theory that light, despite having wave properties, is made up of packets of energy particles (photons). The ability to transform sunlight into electricity is also based on this effect.

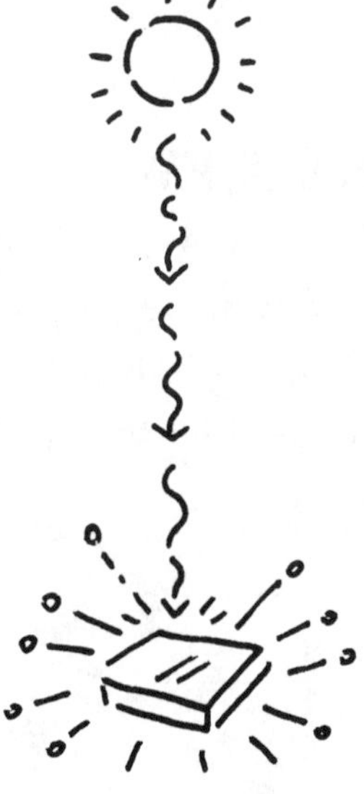

PHOTON

This is a packet of energy particles that makes up light, as suggested by Einstein in 1905.

PHYSICS

For the ancient Greeks, this was the science that sought to explain the essential nature of things. Today physics tries to discover the laws that govern the extremely large (the universe) and the extremely small (the inside of atoms).

PLANCK, MAX

(1858–1947) A German physicist who was the first to formulate the idea of quanta (packets of energy particles), which was then picked up and carried forward by Albert Einstein.

QUANTUM

According to modern physics, these are packets of energy particles which are the basic constituents of matter.

TO BE OR
NOT TO BE
A PARTICLE,
THAT IS
THE
PROBLEM!

QUANTUM MECHANICS

A branch of physics that studies and explains the behavior of the quantum energy particles. It explains it statistically, using probability. Albert Einstein did not always approve of this method.

QUANTUM THEORY

A modern physical theory that mathematically (and statistically) explains the laws governing the multitude of particles and non-particles that populate the subatomic world. Throughout the second part of his life, Einstein tried to connect his theory and this new understanding of physics. Currently every new discovery in the field of quantum represents a further step toward a unified theory of the four forces of nature: gravitational, electromagnetic, strong interactional, weak interactional.

RIEMANN, BERNHARD

(1826–1866) A German mathematician. He introduced the idea of a non-Euclidean geometry in which planes and lines curve, where corners have more dimensions, and where two parallel things can meet again and again. His work influenced Albert Einstein in his description of the universe.

RUSSELL, BERTRAND

(1872–1970) An English mathematician and philosopher. He constantly fought against dictators and for nuclear disarmament. Einstein addressed his last letter to him.

SPACE-TIME TUNNELS

According to physicists, it's possible to pass between the past universe and the future one, thanks to the "curvature of the universe." But while it's theoretically possible, it is very unlikely we can really do it.

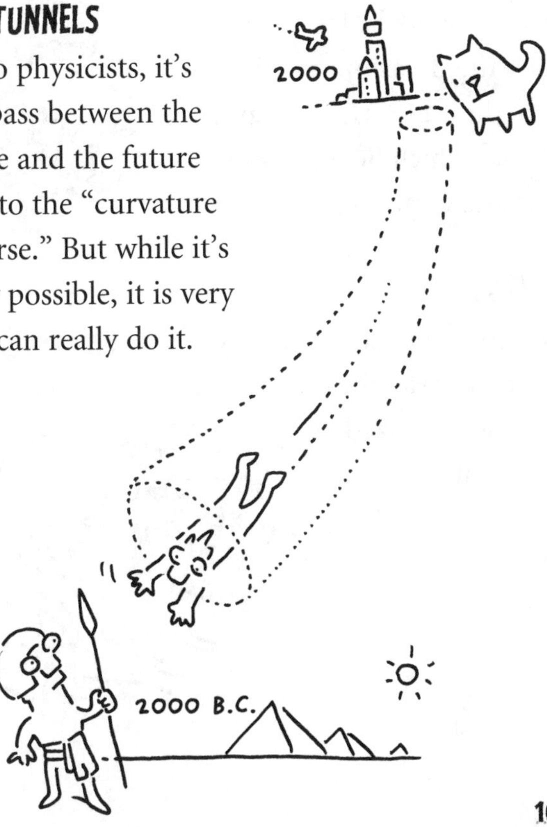

SPEED OF LIGHT

This is constant in the universe. It corresponds to the remarkable speed of almost 186,000 miles per second (300,000 km/second). Recent studies have shown that it can be overtaken.

STYLE

Albert Einstein said his hair was cut in a "shabby style." He loathed wearing socks and his favorite footwear was a pair of sandals. However, when the occasion called for it, he didn't refuse to wear a tuxedo, which he wore with a natural elegance.

SUCCESS

Einstein never chased it. In fact, he was always genuinely amazed at his popularity.

. . . DON'T TRY TO BECOME A MAN OF SUCCESS
. . . BUT A MAN OF VALUE.

SZILARD, LEO

(1898–1964) A Hungarian nuclear physicist. In the United States he took part in the Manhattan Project and saw the first atomic bombs explode. He was always strongly against using atomic weapons for military purposes.

THEORY OF RELATIVITY

In reality, Einstein wanted to call it by a less intriguing name: the Theory of Invariance. It was Max Planck who called it the Theory of Relativity.

THE TIME MACHINE

A novel by Herbert George Wells, published in 1895. He described the 20th century in a discouraging way. He said that the people "will be clearly divided into two levels and two castes. A brutalized and miserable worker class will live underground, while a class of ignorant puppets will live above ground."

TIME TRAVEL

Taking a journey into the future is possible. You just need to go very fast, perhaps aboard a craft traveling close to the speed of light. To go back into the past, on the other hand, is quite unlikely. The only possibility that we can imagine today would be inspired by quantum mechanics. The time machines used by the characters in Crichton's novel, *Timeline*, go back to the past by traveling on a wave of quantum "foam." But there is an open question in that novel: are they really going back in time, or are they being transferred to a parallel past of another universe, one of the infinite universes possible?

UNIVERSE

Humans see and k. about only a small pa. the universe. The theory that it was formed after the Big Bang is now the most widely accepted.

URANIUM

Thanks to its atomic instability, this element is used to start a nuclear reaction where a portion of matter is transformed into energy. The isotope uranium-235, together with plutonium-239, are the main raw materials of the atom bomb.

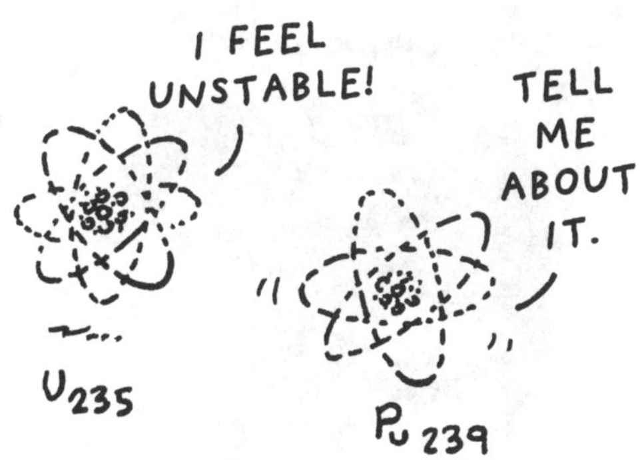

…e piano, but he mostly played the …alled his violin "Lina," and he learned to play …en he was very young. When he died, it was given to his grandson Bernhard.

Illustration by Frank Bruna

LUCA NOVELLI

Writer, artist, journalist. He is the author of books about science and nature that have been translated across the world. He has collaborated with the Italian television company, Rai, with WWF, and with museums and universities. He wrote and directed the *Lampi di Genio in TV* (*Flashes of Genius on TV*) show for Rai Educational (www.lampidigenio.it).

He won the Legambiente (League for the Environment) award in 2001 and the Andersen Prize for popularizing science in 2004.

FLASHES OF GENIUS

A series of biographies of the great scientists—all written and illustrated by Luca Novelli—told in the voice of the protagonist. It is a fun and engaging way to approach science and to get to know the great masters that changed the history of mankind. The series won the Legambiente award in 2004.

FLASHES OF GENIUS

Darwin
and the True Story of the Dinosaurs

When Charles Darwin published *The Origin of Species* in 1859, he shocked the world. In it he claimed that humans were just another animal species that had evolved from more primitive life forms. Years earlier, Darwin had collected thousands of animal specimens during a five-year voyage around the world, specimens that he used to make his case for biologic evolution through natural selection. *Darwin and the True Story of the Dinosaurs* tells the story of the brilliant naturalist who changed humankind's understanding of its origins.

Trade paper, 128 pages
ISBN: 978-1-61373-873-3
$9.99 (CAN $12.99)
Ages 7 to 10

FLASHES OF GENIUS

Newton
and the Antigravity Formula

In the late 1600s, science was still in its infancy. But that changed in 1687 when professor Isaac Newton published a book describing three laws of motion as well as a theory of universal gravitation. He also came up with a brand new field of mathematics, called calculus, to explain it all. The same equations that described the motion of a falling apple could also be used to describe the orbit of planets around the sun. It was revolutionary! *Newton and the Antigravity Formula* tells the story of the man who launched the field of modern physics and changed the way humans look at the world around them.

Trade paper, 112 pages
ISBN: 978-1-61373-861-0
$9.99 (CAN $12.99)
Ages 7 to 10

FLASHES OF GENIUS

Leonardo da Vinci
and the Pen That Drew the Future

Like nobody before or since, Leonardo da Vinci united both the arts and the sciences. He was not only a painter and skilled draftsman but also an inventor and tireless researcher. His art, including the *Mona Lisa* and *The Last Supper*, remain classic of Western civilization. And though he lived 500 years ago, many of his futuristic ideas, such as the contact lens and the armored vehicle, are still with us today. *Leonardo da Vinci and the Pen That Drew the Future* tells the story of the greatest thinker of the Renaissance.

Trade paper, 112 pages
ISBN: 978-1-61373-869-6
$9.99 (CAN $12.99)
Ages 7 to 10